Cybersecurity Mastery

The Complete Guide to Safeguarding Digital Assets

Taylor Royce

DEDICATION

To the unrelenting guardians of the digital realm those who toil away in the background to protect us from online dangers.

To the cybersecurity mentors, educators, and trailblazers who encourage others to strive for greatness, honesty, and expertise in order to protect our digital future.

And to my loved ones, whose steadfast encouragement keeps me motivated in this career.

This book is dedicated to all of you who support a more secure and safe online environment for all. I appreciate your perseverance and commitment.

CONTENTS

ACKNOWLEDGMENTS

Without the inspiration, direction, and help of numerous amazing people, this book would not have been possible.

First and foremost, I want to thank my family and friends for their unfailing support, which has been a continual source of strength and inspiration. I've been able to give this project my whole attention thanks to your understanding and patience.

I am incredibly appreciative of the cybersecurity specialists and professionals whose knowledge, work, and commitment to the area never cease to amaze me. This book was made possible by their groundbreaking work, and their dedication to expanding cybersecurity knowledge is an inspiration to all those working in this field.

I would like to express my sincere gratitude to my mentors and colleagues who generously shared their knowledge and offered priceless advice and comments during the writing process. Your insight and helpful critique have enhanced this work and motivated me to make it the best it can be.

Finally, I would like to thank all of the readers of this book for putting their faith in this advice. I sincerely hope that this book will be a useful tool for you as you work to become an expert in cybersecurity. By working together, we can make the digital world safer and more robust.

I appreciate everyone's participation in this adventure.

CHAPTER 1

OVERVIEW OF INFORMATION SECURITY

1.1 Cybersecurity Understanding

The meaning and significance of cybersecurity

Cybersecurity is the term used to describe the procedures, methods, and tools used to guard against theft, damage, and unauthorized access to computer networks, systems, and data. It includes anything from software protections to physical security measures, all of which are intended to protect the confidentiality, integrity, and availability (CIA) of digital assets. The importance of cybersecurity has grown in a world where almost every element of daily life from personal communications to financial transactions is becoming more and more digital.

- **Confidentiality:** Ensures that only authorized individuals can access sensitive information.

- **Integrity:** Prevents data from being altered or tampered with without authorization.

- **Availability:** keeps authorized users' access to data and systems dependable.

The exponential rise of data breaches, monetary losses, and reputational harm brought on by cyberattacks has only increased the significance of cybersecurity. Strong cybersecurity measures are now expected of both individuals and businesses as they traverse the ever-changing and increasingly complex digital terrain.

The Cybersecurity Evolution

Over the past few decades, the discipline of cybersecurity has experienced substantial evolution in tandem with the rise and transformation of technology. In order to stop intrusions, early cybersecurity initiatives mostly relied on antivirus software and basic firewalls. But as more people used the internet, cyberthreats changed, necessitating more sophisticated and proactive defenses.

- **1980s and 1990s:** The main focus of the early attempts was to stop viruses and illegal access.

- The 2000s: Stronger encryption and multi-factor authentication were introduced as a result of the growing importance of protecting financial data due to e-commerce.

- **2010s:** Advanced identity verification, behavioral analytics, and endpoint protection were made possible by the new security problems posed by cloud computing and mobile technology.

- **Today:** More clever and flexible security solutions are required since the Internet of Things (IoT) and artificial intelligence (AI) have made a huge, interconnected network susceptible to cyberattacks.

Cybersecurity's Function in Contemporary Companies

Cybersecurity is not merely an IT problem in today's business environment; it is an essential part of corporate strategy. Integrating cybersecurity into company culture reduces risk, protects brand equity, and builds consumer confidence. Cybersecurity is essential to modern enterprises for:

- **Risk management:** Cybersecurity precautions lessen possible losses due to operational interruptions or data breaches.

- **Compliance and Legal Liability:** To safeguard personal data, laws such as the CCPA and GDPR impose strict security requirements.

- **The trust of customers:** Good cybersecurity procedures enhance a brand's reputation by reassuring consumers that their data is secure.

1.2 Cyber Threat Types

Phishing, ransomware, and malware

1. **Malware:** This general word refers to any software that is purposefully made to harm a computer, server, or network. Trojan horses, worms, viruses, and malware are among them. Malware can provide hackers access to an organization's networks, delete files, or steal confidential data.

2. **Phishing:** a prevalent type of social engineering in which hackers deceive victims into divulging private information, frequently by sending emails that seem authentic. The sophistication of phishing assaults is improving, making it harder for consumers to identify them.

3. **Ransomware:** Malware that encrypts a victim's data and requests payment to unlock it is very harmful. Attacks using ransomware have increased, frequently focusing on vital sectors like healthcare, where downtime can have disastrous consequences.

Social engineering and insider threats

- **Intrigued Dangers:** Insider dangers come from within the company, as opposed to external cyber threats. They can be purposeful, like when a hostile insider deliberately tries to breach security, or inadvertent, such when an employee unintentionally exposes data.

- The concept of social engineering This strategy, which frequently gets over technical protections, coerces users into disclosing private information. Pretexting, which involves fabricating a situation, and baiting, which involves providing an alluring offer in order to obtain access, are common examples of social engineering.

New Dangers: IoT and AI Exploits

The use of AI in cyberattacks: AI has strengthened cybersecurity defenses, but it has also given attackers more power. Because AI can automate processes, attackers can create highly targeted spear-phishing campaigns or scale phishing attacks.

- **IoT Exploits:** Since many IoT devices lack built-in security protections, the proliferation of these devices presents serious security challenges. Hackers use IoT exploits to take over devices or use them as entry points onto wider networks.

1.3 The Environment of Cybersecurity

International and Sector-Specific Dangers

Industry-specific cybersecurity dangers differ greatly, and each sector faces unique difficulties depending on the type of data it uses and how it operates.

- **Finance:** Financial institutions are frequently the subject of theft or fraud attacks because they handle sensitive client data and transactions.

- **Healthcare:** The healthcare sector is facing significant cybersecurity challenges as a result of the growing use of digital patient records. Health dangers as well as privacy issues may arise from the theft of medical records.

- **Production and Services:** These industries are frequently the target of assaults that could disrupt supply chains or even result in bodily injury because of industrial control systems.

Regulatory Aspects and Compliance

Governments and industry organizations have implemented strict regulatory frameworks with penalties for non-compliance in response to the increase in cyber dangers. Important regulatory frameworks consist of:

The General Data Protection Regulation (GDPR) establishes stringent guidelines for managing the personal data of EU residents.

The CCPA, or California Consumer Privacy Act: requires companies to reveal their data-sharing policies and gives Californians more control over their data.

In order to avoid fraud and data breaches, the Payment Card Industry Data Security Standard (PCI DSS) establishes security guidelines for businesses that process credit card transactions.

Additionally, it is expected of organizations to follow certain data protection guidelines, document their cybersecurity procedures, and do routine audits. Following these rules not only shields the company from legal action but also increases the trust of its partners and clients.

Governments' Role in Cybersecurity

As both regulators and defenders, governments are essential to cybersecurity. They create programs and structures that support cybersecurity awareness, safeguard vital infrastructure, and offer tools for countering online attacks.

- **The following are the national cybersecurity policies:** In order to protect their digital infrastructure, many nations have created national cybersecurity programs.

- **Public-Private Collaborations:** To improve collective security and share information on cyberthreats, governments frequently work with private groups.

- **Programs for Cyber Defense:** To protect their country from cyberattacks, some governments have specialized cybersecurity departments or agencies, like the U.S. Cybersecurity and Infrastructure Security Agency (CISA).

Knowing cybersecurity means not only being aware of the technology protections but also being aware of how cyber threats are changing and the worldwide regulatory landscape. Organizations' dedication to strong cybersecurity procedures becomes not only a defensive tactic but also a crucial differentiation in the marketplace as they get more digitally savvy.

CHAPTER 2

ATTACK VECTORS AND THE THREAT ENVIRONMENT

2.1 Typical Risks to Cybersecurity

Trojan horses, worms, and viruses

Among the most common and ancient types of harmful software (malware), viruses, worms, and Trojan horses all work in different ways to interfere with, corrupt, or steal data.

- **Viruses:** Malware that affixes itself to a trustworthy program or file and propagates when the host file is run is called a virus. Viruses can endanger critical data, slow down systems, or erase files once they are launched. Viruses are frequently distributed through downloaded files or email attachments because they need human action to propagate (such as opening an infected file).

- **Worms:** Worms, in contrast to viruses, are stand-alone malicious software applications that can replicate themselves and propagate via networks without human assistance. Once within a system, they can overload servers, slow down networks, and use up bandwidth. Worms are extremely disruptive due to their capacity for self-propagation, particularly in business settings where network traffic is necessary for day-to-day operations.

- **The following are trojans:** Trojans, which get their name from the Greek mythological Trojan horse, pose as harmless software while secretly executing destructive operations. Because they think the apps are safe, users unintentionally download Trojan horses. Once installed, they have the ability to install other malware, steal confidential information, or create backdoors for hackers. Trojans are not self-replicating like viruses or worms, yet they are very efficient at targeted attacks because of their deceit.

APTs, or advanced persistent threats

Advanced Persistent Threats (APTs) are complex, protracted attacks that are frequently planned by well funded organizations, including nation-states or organized cybercriminal groups. APTs are made to penetrate high-value targets, such as governmental organizations, banks, or big businesses, in order to obtain intelligence, steal confidential information, or cause long-term disruptions to operations.

- **Stealthy Operations:** APTs employ secret methods to evade detection, like disguising their actions with sophisticated encryption or hiding in plain sight within trustworthy processes.
- **Multistage Approach:** APTs frequently employ a staged approach that consists of reconnaissance, initial exploitation, and grounding themselves in the target's network. After that, attackers can increase their rights and spread laterally throughout the infrastructure of the company.
- **Exfiltration and Maintenance:** APTs are made to stay hidden for extended periods of time, gathering

information over time and relaying it to the attackers without the organization being notified.

Botnets and DDoS Attacks

By overloading a targeted server, service, or network with excessive traffic, Distributed Denial of Service (DDoS) attacks seek to prevent authorized users from accessing the system. DDoS attacks are frequently carried out by botnets, which are networks of infected devices managed remotely. Important traits consist of:

1. **Resource Depletion:** DDoS assaults cause service interruptions by depleting network resources like bandwidth or CPU capacity.
2. **The infrastructure of the botnet:** Thousands of compromised devices, including PCs, Internet of Things devices, and cell phones, can form botnets. These devices work together to send traffic to the target at the same time, overwhelming its defenses.
3. **The following are mitigation challenges:** Because of their size and dispersed nature, DDoS attacks are difficult to defend against. The damage can be

lessened with the use of mitigation techniques including rate limitation, IP filtering, and content delivery networks (CDNs).

2.2 Strategies for Social Engineering

Phishing, Vishing, and Spear Phishing

Social engineering is the practice of manipulating human psychology in order to obtain information or systems without authorization. Social engineering techniques like phishing, spear phishing, and vishing (voice phishing) take advantage of users' trust and ignorance.

- **Phishing:** Phishing attacks are fraudulent emails or communications that pose as reliable organizations, such banks, government offices, or service providers, in an attempt to fool recipients into disclosing private information, opening dangerous attachments, or clicking on links.
- **The Spear Phishing technique:** Spear phishing, in contrast to ordinary phishing, is extremely focused and customized for certain people or organizations.

In order to craft convincing communications, attackers investigate their targets, which makes spear phishing more successful and difficult to identify.

- **Dying:** In order to obtain private information or money, attackers use this tactic to telephone (typically from fake numbers) and pose as authorized representatives of businesses. Tech support scams frequently utilize vishing, in which scammers persuade victims to infect their devices with malware.

Cyberattack Manipulation Techniques

In order to instill a sense of urgency or trust, social engineering uses psychological manipulation tactics. Among the often employed strategies are:

1. **Pretexting:** To win over a target, attackers fabricate a story or situation that seems plausible. They might pose as an IT support agent or bank representative and ask for private information while claiming to be helping the victim.

2. **Baiting:** Attackers lure victims in by offering

incentives or advantages, like a prize or a free download. The victim may unintentionally download malware or divulge sensitive information if they fall for the trick.

3. **Scare Techniques:** Attackers frequently instill anxiety or a sense of urgency in their victims, forcing them to act quickly without first confirming their genuineness. Fake warnings stating that the user's account has been compromised are one example.

Awareness and Prevention Techniques

Organizations and individuals must place a high priority on awareness and education in order to protect against social engineering attacks. Among the successful preventative techniques are:

1. **Employee Training:** Frequent training sessions instruct staff members on how to spot and handle vishing calls, phishing efforts, and other forms of social engineering.

2. By adding an additional layer of security,

Multi-Factor Authentication (MFA) makes it more difficult for attackers to get access to accounts, even if they manage to get their hands on user credentials.

3. **Phishing Campaign Simulations:** Through simulated phishing exercises, feedback, and reinforcement of established practices for handling suspicious messages, organizations can assess employees' knowledge.

2.3 Emerging Technologies' Role

AI in Defense and Cyber Attacks

In cybersecurity, artificial intelligence (AI) has become a double-edged sword that improves both attack and defense strategies.

- **AI in Cyber Defense:** AI-driven security solutions examine vast amounts of data to identify and address irregularities instantly. Traditional security systems could miss questionable activity, but machine learning algorithms can recognize new trends. Real-time fraud detection, automated incident response, and predictive threat analysis are some examples of applications.

- **The use of AI in cyberattacks:** Conversely, AI makes it possible for cybercriminals to launch more complex and swift attacks. Attackers can use AI to automate processes like spear phishing, CAPTCHA circumvention, and password guessing. Furthermore, because AI-driven bots can mimic human behavior, it can be more difficult to identify malicious activities in network traffic or on social media sites.

IoT Challenges and Vulnerabilities

Because linked devices such as wearable technology, industrial sensors, and smart home appliances—are frequently unregulated and unsecure, the Internet of Things (IoT) creates new vulnerabilities.

It is difficult to apply identical protection measures across various manufacturers and device types due to the lack of standardized security standards in IoT devices.

- **Device Vulnerability:** A lot of Internet of Things devices are not built with security in mind, which puts them at risk for things like obsolete firmware, weak passwords, and insufficient encryption. These gadgets are easily exploitable, making them sources of access for criminals.

- **The surface of complex attacks:** Every new gadget increases the number of possible points of entry for hackers, making network monitoring and security more difficult. IoT devices can be compromised by attackers to obtain data, obtain illegal access, or initiate DDoS assaults using botnets such as Mirai.

Cloud Security Risks and Things to Think About

Businesses are using cloud infrastructure more and more because it is flexible and scalable, but it also presents special security concerns that call for certain cloud-native protections.

- **Misconfigurations and Data Breach:** Data breaches, in which private information is unintentionally made available to unauthorized individuals, are frequently caused by improperly configured cloud storage and permissions. Strict access controls must be put in place, and cloud configurations must be routinely audited.

- **Model of Shared Responsibility:** Customers are in charge of protecting their data and apps within the cloud environment, while cloud providers handle infrastructure security under the shared responsibility model. To avoid security flaws, it is crucial to comprehend this separation of duties.

- **Risks of Multiple Tenancies:** Many cloud environments are multi-tenant, which means that the infrastructure is shared by several clients. Vulnerabilities in one tenant's environment could possibly impact others if it is not adequately secured, which could result in cross-tenant breaches or data leaks.

The cybersecurity threat landscape is ever-changing and poses both straightforward and complex problems. Organizations and individuals need to be alert and proactive, from identifying the impact of developing technology to comprehending typical cyberthreats. In this increasingly complicated digital environment, using a layered security approach that integrates policy, education, and technology defenses can help reduce risks and safeguard important assets.

CHAPTER 3

FOUNDATIONS OF NETWORK SECURITY

3.1 Network Security Fundamentals

Protocols and Architecture for Network Security

In order to safeguard network resources from attacks, network security architecture includes the methodical design and use of security policies, controls, and protocols. A strategic foundation for guaranteeing data availability, confidentiality, and integrity across all networked systems and services is provided by this architecture.

- **Layered Defense**: A layered or "defense-in-depth" strategy is commonly used in network security architecture, wherein several security measures are applied across several network tiers to establish redundancy. Firewalls, intrusion detection/prevention systems, and access control methods are frequently found in layers.

- **Protocols:** Encrypting data transfers is made possible by essential network protocols including Secure Sockets Layer (SSL), Transport Layer Security (TLS), and IP Security (IPsec). Protocols for virtual private networks (VPNs), such OpenVPN and L2TP/IPsec, safeguard data while it moves between distant users and the network.

IDS/IPS Systems, VPNs, and firewalls

These technologies are necessary for traffic monitoring, network boundary security, and preventing unwanted access.

- **Firewalls:** The first line of protection is a firewall, which filters outgoing and incoming traffic according to pre-established security rules. The packet-filtering firewall (Layer 3, Network) and the application-layer firewall (Layer 7, Application) are two examples of the several layers at which firewalls function. Firewalls can be set up to enforce security regulations throughout the entire enterprise, block harmful communications, and limit unauthorized access.

- **Virtual Private Networks, or VPNs:** By establishing encrypted "tunnels" between the user's device and the network, virtual private networks (VPNs) allow for safe remote access to a private network. VPNs are especially useful in settings where employees operate remotely since they encrypt data to prevent interception and guarantee data integrity and privacy.

- **Intrusion Detection and Prevention Systems, or IDS/IPS:** IDS systems keep an eye on network traffic for indications of questionable activity and notify administrators when something seems off. By actively preventing or lessening identified threats, IPS systems go one step further. IDS/IPS systems look for possible threats like port scans or malware infection by analyzing patterns, signatures, and abnormalities in traffic.

Zoning and Network Segmentation

In order to control access and minimize possible dangers,

network segmentation entails breaking a network up into smaller, isolated zones or segments.

- **Zoning:** Zones, like the Demilitarized Zone (DMZ), separate sensitive internal networks from services that are visible to the public. Without exposing the entire network to possible attackers, the DMZ permits external access to essential services (such as a web server).

- **Micro-Segmentation:** Micro-segmentation is a sophisticated technique that uses firewalls or access controls at the workload level to create extremely granular zones within a data center or cloud environment. This restricts an attacker's ability to travel laterally within a network, even in the event that one segment is compromised.

Because rules like PCI-DSS require that payment processing zones be kept apart from other parts of the network, segmentation reduces the harm that a breach can cause, prevents attackers from moving laterally, and makes compliance management more effective.

3.2 Protecting Network Equipment

Safeguarding Firewalls, Switches, and Routers

Since routers, switches, and firewalls are the foundation of network infrastructure, their security is crucial to preserving the network's overall integrity.

Because they control the flow of data between networks, routers are often the subject of attacks. Updating firmware, turning off unwanted services, creating secure passwords, and putting IPsec or SSL VPNs in place for remote access are all part of router security.

- **Switches:** Switches manage traffic in a local network by operating at the data connection layer (Layer 2). Configuring port security, turning on MAC filtering, turning off unused ports, and turning on VLANs to restrict broadcast domains are all part of securing switches.

- **Firewalls:** Risks can be reduced by keeping stringent access control procedures and updating firewall firmware on a regular basis. To make sure they meet organizational demands and legal requirements, firewall rules should be reviewed on a regular basis.

ACL (Access Control List) Configuration

In order to control incoming and outgoing network traffic according to IP addresses, protocols, and ports, routers, switches, and firewalls use sets of rules called access control lists, or ACLs.

- **Ingress and Egress Filtering:** While egress ACLs limit outgoing traffic to stop potentially dangerous transmissions, ingress ACLs filter incoming traffic to stop unwanted access.
- **The specificity of the rule:** By default, ACLs should block all other traffic and only let required traffic, making them as detailed as feasible. A "deny-all" policy with certain "allow" exceptions lessens the likelihood of unwanted access.

ACL deployment across several network layers, such as the router, switch, and firewall, guarantees redundant protection and reduces the possibility of unintentional access.

Wireless Network Security

Because wireless networks are susceptible to interception and unauthorized access, they need specific security measures.

- To protect data and prevent unwanted access, it is essential to make sure that all wireless networks are using Wi-Fi Protected Access 3 (WPA3) encryption, the newest and most secure protocol.
- Enabling MAC address filtering prevents unauthorized devices from connecting to the network by limiting access to only known devices.
- **Network segmentation and hidden SSID:** It is harder for attackers to find the network when the SSID is hidden. Furthermore, separating wireless networks for visitors and staff lowers the possibility of internal threats and facilitates improved network administration.

3.3 Tracking and Identifying Incidents

Analysis of Network Traffic

In order to find indications of malicious behavior, network traffic analysis (NTA) continuously examines data packets as they move across the network. Metrics including packet size, connection patterns, and bandwidth utilization are tracked by NTA solutions.

- **Traffic Baseline Creation:** Organizations can promptly identify anomalies, like unexpected traffic surges or odd IP addresses, by creating a baseline of normal network traffic.

- In order to detect dangerous payloads in traffic, including malware or phishing attempts, Deep Packet Inspection (DPI) is a handy tool that examines the contents of data packets rather than just their headers.

- **Advantages:** Real-time traffic analysis improves visibility into network activities, facilitates quicker threat response, and offers early identification of possible assaults.

Techniques for Detecting Anomalies

In network security, anomaly detection finds odd trends or actions that differ from predetermined standards. Anomaly detection assists in identifying small risks that signature-based approaches could overlook by combining statistical and machine learning-based techniques.

- The use of statistical methods These methods identify typical traffic patterns using statistical models and sound an alarm when they deviate. Calculating means and variances for particular metrics, such as network flow or bandwidth utilization, is one example.

- **Algorithms for Machine Learning:** Due to its ability to identify subtle, unidentified threats and adjust to changing network patterns, machine learning-based anomaly detection is becoming more and more popular. Clustering and anomaly scoring are examples of unsupervised learning methods that can identify anomalous traffic without the need for pre-established labels or criteria.

- **Applications in the Real World**: APTs, insider threats, and zero-day assaults are examples of advanced threats that can be detected with the use of anomaly detection. By decreasing false positives and concentrating more on real threats, it also improves the overall accuracy of security monitoring.

Real-Time Monitoring with SIEM

Systems for Security Information and Event Management (SIEM) combine information from several networks to offer thorough real-time security event monitoring, correlation, and analysis.

- **Correlation and Data Aggregation:** SIEM platforms gather information from a number of sources, including network logs, firewalls, IDS/IPS systems, and endpoint devices. After that, they link these occurrences, highlighting trends that can point to a planned attack or questionable behavior.
- **Real-time reporting and alerting:** When certain security events, such persistent login failures or data exfiltration attempts, take place, SIEM solutions send out real-time notifications. This guarantees that IT security teams can react swiftly to lessen possible

risks.

- **Forensics and Incident Investigation:** SIEM logs can offer crucial information for forensic investigation in the case of an incident, assisting teams in tracking down the attacker's movements, locating exploited vulnerabilities, and determining the extent of the assault.

Protecting digital assets from an expanding range of attacks requires a grasp of and adherence to basic network security principles. Organizations must take a holistic approach to network security, from building a strong security architecture to guaranteeing strict device protection and ongoing monitoring. Building on the fundamental understanding of network security fundamentals, the upcoming chapter will explore more sophisticated security procedures.

CHAPTER 4

Access Control and Endpoint Security

Two of the most important elements of contemporary cybersecurity frameworks are endpoint security and access control. Endpoints like laptops, mobile devices, and desktop computers are becoming more and more vulnerable as network perimeters grow and more workers work remotely. In order to provide a thorough cyber defense, this chapter will examine the fundamentals of identity and access management, endpoint security, and the new Zero Trust model.

4.1 Essentials of Endpoint Security

Endpoint detection, antivirus, and anti-malware software

The fundamental tools for defending endpoints against ransomware, malicious code, and other types of malware that jeopardize device integrity and data security are antivirus and anti-malware software.

- **Antivirus:** Conventional antivirus software looks for threats using a database of known malware signatures. Signature-based antivirus software is useful against typical threats, but it has drawbacks, especially when it comes to identifying novel or unidentified malware strains.

- **Anti-Malware:** Compared to typical antivirus software, anti-malware programs offer more comprehensive protection. They frequently use behavioral analysis to identify anomalous system or application actions that could be signs of infection. This method makes it possible to identify dangers that traditional antivirus programs might overlook, such as malware, adware, and rootkits.

EDR stands for Endpoint Detection and Response. By offering real-time monitoring, threat detection, and automated responses across all endpoints, EDR goes beyond antivirus and anti-malware software. EDR solutions enable quicker reaction times by continuously gathering data to spot questionable activities. Advanced persistent threats (APTs) and other sophisticated attack methods are especially successfully countered by EDR systems.

Configuration and Device Hardening

Through the reduction of potential attack routes, device hardening lessens an endpoint's vulnerability to cyber attacks. It entails setting up the firmware, apps, and operating system to improve security.

- **Configuration Standards:** It is crucial to create and preserve baseline configurations for every device. Disabling unnecessary services, altering default passwords, and turning on operating system security features are examples of secure configuration techniques.
- **Operating System Hardening:** The key to hardening is making sure operating systems have the most recent security updates installed and making use of features like firewall settings, network protections, and access limits.
- **Hardening of Applications:** Attackers have fewer

possible avenues of access when applications are restricted to those required for the organization's activities. While eliminating pointless apps lowers risks, application whitelisting and restricted user access improve security.

Endpoint Detection and Response's (EDR) Function

Because EDR systems combine automatic response, detection, and monitoring into a single system, they are essential to endpoint security.

- EDR systems provide continuous monitoring, which is essential for spotting irregularities as they occur. They examine endpoint events in search of trends like odd login attempts or permission escalations that point to an attack.

- **Autonomous Reactions:** To stop attacks from moving laterally, EDR solutions can automatically isolate compromised endpoints. Additionally, they cause alert messages, which provide IT professionals with instant notice of possible security breaches.

- **The ability to hunt threats:** Proactive threat

hunting is supported by many EDR platforms, which enables security analysts to look for indicators of compromise (IoCs) throughout the environment. EDR improves the organization's overall threat readiness by identifying possible threats before they materialize.

4.2 Management of Identity and Access (IAM)

Authentication and Authorization as IAM Principles

Controlling user access to corporate systems, data, and applications requires Identity and Access Management (IAM). It enforces rules on who is allowed to use what resources and when.

- **Verification:** Before allowing access, authentication confirms users' identities. Passwords, biometric scanning, and token-based systems are examples of common techniques.
- **Permission:** Authorization establishes the user's level of access after authentication. In order to guarantee that users have only the access required

for their job duties, authorization policies are frequently based on roles and security groups.

- **Tools and Protocols for IAM:** To simplify access control across systems, IAM solutions frequently incorporate protocols like LDAP and SAML along with capabilities like identity federation and single sign-on (SSO). By reducing the requirement for multiple application logins, these technologies increase efficiency.

The Best Practices for Multi-Factor Authentication (MFA)

Secure IAM systems must have multi-factor authentication (MFA), which adds an additional degree of security by requiring several types of identification to validate a user's identity.

- **Best Practices:** Combining the user's knowledge (password), possessions (mobile device), and identity (biometric data) is a key component of an effective MFA solution.
- **Time-Based One-Time Passwords (TOTP):** TOTP

techniques increase security without sacrificing usability by generating time-sensitive codes that users must enter after entering their password.

- **Token-Based and Biometric Authentication:** For more robust authentication, many businesses use physical tokens or biometrics (such as fingerprint or facial recognition). Token-based MFA is especially useful in settings like financial services or health care that demand a high level of security.

The implementation of flexible rules, such as adaptive or context-aware MFA, which evaluates risk variables like login location or device, helps to combine security requirements with a seamless user experience. This is because MFA can occasionally cause friction for users.

Role-Based Access Control (RBAC) Implementation

By strategically controlling user permissions according to job functions, Role-Based Access Control (RBAC) makes sure that people have access to only the data required to carry out their duties.

Roles are assigned to users, and these roles determine their access permissions. For instance, while HR professionals can view employee records, finance staff can only access financial data. Unauthorized data access can be avoided by clearly defining these responsibilities and permissions.

- **Least Privilege and Hierarchy:** RBAC functions according to a hierarchy in which access privileges are restricted according to necessity. The least privilege principle, which limits users to the bare minimum of rights necessary for their tasks, is supported by this.

- **Scalability and Auditing:** RBAC makes access control easier, especially for big businesses. The technology helps firms meet compliance standards by maintaining records for auditing purposes and facilitating the easy updating of role assignments when responsibilities change.

4.3 Architecture of Zero Trust

The Zero Trust Principles

The foundation of the Zero Trust security paradigm is the idea that businesses shouldn't blindly trust anyone within or outside of their boundaries. Rather, it necessitates ongoing verification for every access request, regardless of where they come from.

- **"Never Trust, Always Verify":** Zero Trust needs identity verification, device security checks, and access controls to be checked every time since it believes that every access request is a possible threat.

- **Least Privilege Access and Micro-Segmentation:** In order to minimize the "blast radius" in the event that an attacker gains access, the Zero Trust model depends on micro-segmentation, which involves separating network segments and implementing security policies for each segment.

- **Ongoing Observation:** Zero Trust requires constant monitoring of all network operations and access attempts, in contrast to typical security models that only monitor at entry points. This allows for the prompt identification and handling of unusual activity.

Putting Least Privilege Access into Practice

In keeping with Zero Trust's focus on lowering access-related risk, the principle of least privilege guarantees that users and devices have only the minimal access required for their jobs.

- **Granular Permissions:** To keep people from accessing systems beyond their responsibilities, least privilege necessitates precisely calibrated access control, frequently down to the file or application level.

- **Adaptive Access Policies:** By dynamically modifying permissions, context-aware access policies where access is allowed or prohibited according to user identity, location, and device status support least privilege.

- **Periodic Access Reviews:** Frequent audits of user access rights allow for prompt modifications by identifying situations in which access levels are excessively broad. In order to preserve compliance and stop privilege creep, these assessments are essential.

The Benefits and Difficulties of Zero Trust

Although implementing Zero Trust has many security benefits, its successful implementation also necessitates careful planning and resources.

Benefits:

1. **Enhanced Security Posture:** By implementing stringent access controls, Zero Trust restricts the extent of data breaches and lowers the possibility of attackers moving laterally within the network.

2. **Better Visibility and Control:** Ongoing authentication and monitoring give more insight into how users and devices behave, which facilitates the identification and handling of questionable activities.

3. **Compliance and Risk Management:** By adhering to strict access control, Zero Trust helps firms fulfill compliance standards with data privacy and security laws.

The adoption of a Zero Trust model frequently necessitates substantial adjustments to current network architectures, identity verification procedures, and security guidelines.

Implementing Zero Trust may need a significant amount of resources, including strong IAM systems, ongoing monitoring tools, and an all-encompassing endpoint management plan.

At first, users used to more conventional access mechanisms can find Zero Trust inconvenient. The shift can be facilitated by gradual implementation and clear communication.

Access control and endpoint security are essential for preserving organizational security in a threat landscape that is becoming more complicated. Organizations may defend against internal and external threats by combining advanced models like Zero Trust, powerful endpoint defenses, and strong IAM procedures. The following chapter will concentrate on data protection tactics and industry best practices for safeguarding confidential data throughout the company.

CHAPTER 5

SECURITY OF APPLICATIONS

Application security has become crucial in today's threat landscape to protect sensitive data, maintain system integrity, and uphold user confidence. Applications are particularly vulnerable to cyberattacks since they act as direct interfaces to data and network infrastructure. In order to build strong application defense systems, this chapter examines the principles of application security with an emphasis on vulnerabilities, best practices, and proactive testing techniques.

5.1 Overview of Security for Applications

The procedures and resources used to secure software applications during their development, deployment, and operation are collectively referred to as application security. By taking a proactive stance, the chances of vulnerabilities that an attacker could exploit are decreased.

OWASP Top 10 Common Application Vulnerabilities

The OWASP Top 10 is a basic reference for developers and security experts, representing a consensus on the most important security threats in web applications. The first step in creating secure apps is being aware of these risks:

- When untrusted data (such as SQL, NoSQL, LDAP, or OS commands) is provided to an interpreter, it might lead to injection flaws, which could allow attackers to alter queries or run unauthorized commands.

- **Broken Authentication and Session Management:** When credentials or session tokens are not correctly managed, these vulnerabilities may result in unauthorized access.

- **Cross-Site Scripting (XSS):** Allows hackers to insert harmful scripts into other users' web sites, jeopardizing sensitive data and session data.

- Applications that reveal internal implementation details give attackers the opportunity to alter object references and get unauthorized access to resources.

This is known as "Insecure Direct Object References" (IDOR).

- **Security Misconfiguration:** Exploitable vulnerabilities are created by improperly configured settings or default credentials in systems and apps.

- **Sensitive Data Exposure**: Inadequate security measures and poor encryption can allow unwanted access to private information.

- Attackers utilize Cross-Site Request Forgery (CSRF) to fool authenticated users into sending requests on behalf of their sessions, which might result in unexpected consequences.

- It is possible for attackers to take advantage of security holes introduced by outdated libraries and dependencies.

- **Inadequate Logging and Monitoring:** The discovery of breaches may be delayed if important events are not logged or application behavior is not observed.

Software Development Life Cycle (SDLC) Security

A "security-first" culture is established by integrating

security into each stage of the Software Development Life Cycle (SDLC), which lowers vulnerabilities and makes it possible to identify any problems early.

- **Requirements Gathering:** To guarantee that security requirements are fulfilled throughout development, identify them early in the project. This entails establishing unambiguous access controls and adhering to data protection laws.
- Integrate threat modeling and security design evaluations with an emphasis on data encryption, safe authentication, and authorization procedures.
- **Coding:** Vulnerabilities are decreased by using secure coding techniques. To find problems early, developers should use secure libraries, coding standards, and static code analysis.
- **Testing**: To verify security controls, security testing, such as vulnerability assessments, penetration testing, and code reviews, should be carried out.
- **Deployment and Maintenance**: To ensure that applications remain secure after deployment, continuous security monitoring, patch management, and logging procedures are necessary.

Protective Coding Techniques

During development, secure coding techniques shield apps against exploitable flaws:

- **Sanitization and Input Validation:** Sanitize data to eliminate harmful content and enforce input validation to stop injection attacks.
- **Error Handling:** Don't let error messages divulge private information. Error messages ought to be generic and should only log specific information on the server side.
- Role-based access control (RBAC), multi-factor authentication (MFA), and strong password policies should all be enforced in order to prevent unwanted access.
- **Code Audits and Reviews:** Finding errors in code can be aided by regular peer and security expert reviews. Static analysis is one example of an automated tool that can identify vulnerabilities.

5.2 Security of Web and Mobile Applications

Due to their disparate contexts, platforms, and threat characteristics, online and mobile applications require different approaches to security. Mobile applications run on user-controlled devices, although web applications are frequently more accessible and publicly visible.

API Security and Web Application Firewalls (WAF)

By examining HTTP/S traffic and thwarting harmful requests, Web Application Firewalls (WAFs) play a critical role in filtering, monitoring, and safeguarding web applications from a variety of threats.

- **WAF:** A WAF serves as a security barrier, permitting valid requests but preventing malicious traffic. It finds and stops typical attacks like SQL injection and cross-site scripting by examining incoming and outgoing HTTP/S traffic.

API Security: While APIs facilitate data transfers across systems, they also make endpoints vulnerable to intrusions. Protecting APIs entails:

- **Authentication and Authorization:** Limit API access by using tokens like OAuth or JWT.
- Limiting the number of API calls a client can make helps prevent denial-of-service (DoS) attacks.
- **Input Validation:** Verify and clean all data given to APIs to avoid injection attacks.

Mobile App Risks and Weaknesses

Because mobile applications are used on a variety of devices with different security settings, they provide particular risks and challenges:

- Sensitive information is frequently kept locally by mobile apps, which leaves it vulnerable to theft if left unencrypted.
- **Inadequate Transport Layer Security:** Mobile applications may be vulnerable to man-in-the-middle attacks if they use unencrypted communication.
- **Weak Authentication Mechanisms:** Unauthorized access may result from inadequate session management procedures or from the absence of multi-factor authentication.

- **Device Vulnerabilities:** Older OS versions or weak third-party apps on mobile devices might expose apps to dangers that are out of the developer's control.

Developing Secure Mobile Applications

To reduce these threats, secure mobile app development uses specific security procedures:

- **Data Encryption:** To prevent unwanted access, encrypt critical data while it's in transit and locally stored.
- **Device Fingerprinting and Biometrics**: To increase security, incorporate biometrics or device-based identification.

To fix new vulnerabilities and keep programs compatible with current OS versions, make sure they receive regular security updates.

5.3 Vulnerability assessment and penetration testing

Organizations employ proactive techniques like penetration

testing and vulnerability assessments to find and fix application flaws before hackers can take advantage of them.

Penetration testing types and stages

Penetration testing evaluates a system, network, or application's security protections by simulating an attack.

- **Black Box Testing:** In order to find vulnerabilities, testers simulate an external attack without having any prior knowledge of the internal operations of the application.
- **White Box Testing:** Because testers are fully conversant with the infrastructure and code of the application, possible vulnerabilities can be thoroughly examined.
- The hybrid technique known as "gray box testing" allows testers to concentrate on areas that are more susceptible to assault because they have only partial knowledge.

Penetration Testing Stages:

1. **Planning and Reconnaissance:** Establish the goals

and scope of the testing as well as obtain information about the application to replicate real-world situations.

2. **Scanning and Analysis:** Map the application environment and find exposed ports, services, and possible attack points using scanning tools.

3. **Exploitation:** Test vulnerabilities by trying to exploit them and confirming their effect and possible outcomes.

4. **Reporting and Post-Exploitation:** Following testing, security teams examine the findings, record vulnerabilities, and suggest corrective actions.

Vulnerability Scanning Methods and Tools

Compared to penetration testing, vulnerability scanning solutions provide a less invasive baseline level of security evaluation by automating the identification of potential security flaws.

- Nessus, Qualys, and OpenVAS are examples of automated scanning tools that check networks and applications for known vulnerabilities and provide a list of problems found.

- **Methods of Manual Testing:** By confirming vulnerabilities found and looking for intricate problems that scanners might overlook, manual testing can be used in conjunction with automatic scanning.

- **Regular Scanning Frequency:** Making time for daily, weekly, or monthly vulnerability scans guarantees that new vulnerabilities are found and fixed as soon as possible.

Risk Evaluation and Remedial Techniques

Organizations must evaluate and rank risks according to their seriousness, possible consequences, and probability of exploitation after detecting vulnerabilities.

- Every vulnerability should be categorized according to its level of criticality, with high-severity vulnerabilities being given priority for prompt remedy.

- **Patching and remediation**: Patching or resetting the impacted systems will fix vulnerabilities.

High-risk vulnerabilities must be patched right away, although lower-priority problems might be fixed gradually.

The ongoing process of improvement Testing results are used to improve security procedures, coding standards, and training programs in an efficient application security program.

Application security is a complex field that needs to be considered throughout the entire software development and deployment process. Organizations can greatly improve their application security posture by comprehending and putting into practice secure coding techniques, establishing safeguards for web and mobile applications, and regularly performing penetration testing and vulnerability assessments. In addition to preventing data breaches, this proactive strategy improves consumer confidence and complies with regulations. The importance of encryption and data security in protecting sensitive data in applications and larger IT systems will be covered in the upcoming chapter.

CHAPTER 6

ENCRYPTION AND DATA SECURITY

Although data is one of an organization's most precious assets, it is becoming more and more susceptible to various risks. Implementing strong encryption techniques and following strict security procedures are necessary to guarantee the availability, confidentiality, and integrity of data. This chapter examines the usage of encryption and cryptography, dives into basic data protection concepts, and emphasizes the significance of Data Loss Prevention (DLP) in data security.

6.1 Principles of Data Protection

Sensitive information must be identified, secured, and managed throughout its lifecycle using an organized method for effective data security. Organizations can use the fundamental framework provided by data protection principles to safeguard information assets and guarantee regulatory compliance.

Data Classification and Sensitivity Levels

Data classification is the process of grouping information according to its level of sensitivity and security needs. This procedure is crucial for figuring out which data assets are important and how secure each category has to be.

- **Categories of Classification:** Based on variables including sensitivity, legal requirements, and the possible consequences of a breach, organizations usually divide data into categories like public, internal, confidential, and restricted.
- **Levels of Sensitivity:** Organizations can prioritize security measures by assigning sensitivity levels to data. Financial records, health information, intellectual property, and personally identifiable information (PII) are all considered sensitive data and need to be protected more thoroughly.

To guarantee that only authorized workers have access to sensitive data, access controls are designed with classification and sensitivity levels in mind. Additionally, these restrictions make it easier to comply with privacy laws like the CCPA and GDPR.

Obfuscation, anonymization, and data masking

Techniques like data masking, anonymization, and obfuscation can assist in safeguarding sensitive data, particularly when it's utilized in settings like analytics or testing where complete access to the data isn't required.

- By substituting fake data with the same structure for the original data, **Data Masking:** enables users to complete tasks without disclosing actual information. A camouflaged credit card number might appear, for instance, as 1234-5678-XXXX-XXXX.
- Anonymization is the process of permanently deleting identifiable information from datasets so that it cannot be linked to a specific person. In order to preserve individual privacy, this method is frequently employed in research and analysis.
- **Obfuscation:** Modifies data in a way that is either irreversible or reversible, making it hard to use or

comprehend without specific knowledge. Sensitive information can be obscured without compromising data integrity in application development and testing.

Safe Data Backup and Storage Procedures

In the event of data breaches, system malfunctions, or natural disasters, data storage and backup procedures are essential to guaranteeing data availability and integrity.

- **Encryption at Rest:** Data kept on disk can be encrypted to prevent unwanted access in the event that the storage media is compromised. Data at rest can be secured via full-disk encryption or file-level encryption.
- **Controls over Storage Device Access:** Unauthorized data access is reduced when role-based access control (RBAC) is used to restrict access to storage systems.

Data accessibility is guaranteed even in the event of system failure or physical damage to local systems when backup data is encrypted and stored offsite or in a secure cloud environment.

6.2 Cryptography and Encryption

By safeguarding data while it is in transit and at rest, encryption and cryptography serve as the foundation of data security. Encryption guarantees that even if data is intercepted, it cannot be accessed without the right decryption keys by converting it into unintelligible formats.

Encryption: Symmetric and Asymmetric

Data is secured using two primary forms of encryption: symmetric and asymmetric. Depending on the kind of data and the setting, each offers unique benefits and applications.

- One key is used for both encryption and decryption in symmetric encryption. It is well-known for its effectiveness and speed, making it perfect for full-disk encryption and other massive data encryption applications. However, since the sender and recipient need to share the same key, secure key exchange is necessary.

- AES (Advanced Encryption Standard), DES (Data Encryption Standard), and Blowfish are examples of algorithms.

- A public key is used for encryption, and a private key is used for decryption, in asymmetric encryption. Although it is slower than symmetric encryption, this technique is frequently used for digital signatures and secure communications.

- RSA (Rivest-Shamir-Adleman), ECC (Elliptic Curve Cryptography), and Diffie-Hellman key exchange are a few examples of algorithms.

PKI Infrastructure and Key Management

Since poorly managed keys can result in illegal data access, effective key management is essential to preserving encryption security.

- The risk of key compromise is decreased by securely keeping keys in Hardware Security Modules (HSMs) and rotating them on a regular basis.

- **PKI Infrastructure:** Public Key Infrastructure

(PKI) controls the creation, sharing, and revocation of digital certificates, enabling encryption and digital signatures. PKI links public keys to validated entities, facilitating trusted communication.

In order to verify the identification of people or organizations, PKI depends on Certificate Authorities (CA) to issue digital certificates. For PKI to remain trustworthy, CA management must be done correctly.

New Developments in Cryptography and Quantum-Safe Encryption

Traditional encryption algorithms may become insecure as processing power rises, especially with the introduction of quantum computing. This has led to the creation of quantum-safe encryption methods.

- **Quantum-Safe Algorithms:** To protect data in the post-quantum era, algorithms that are immune to quantum computer attacks, like hash-based and lattice-based cryptography, are being developed.
- **Homomorphic Encryption:** Enables secure data processing in delicate applications such as financial

analysis and cloud computing by allowing computation on encrypted data without the need for decryption.

- **Zero-Knowledge Proofs:** These cryptographic proofs, which are helpful in privacy-preserving authentication systems, enable one party to demonstrate the truth of a statement without disclosing any underlying knowledge.

6.3 Preventing Data Loss (DLP)

The term "Data Loss Prevention" (DLP) refers to the methods and instruments used by businesses to stop sensitive data from being accessed, used, or transmitted without authorization. By putting DLP procedures in place, data is safeguarded against unintentional or deliberate leaks.

DLP Implementation and Strategies

Understanding data flows, spotting high-risk regions, and putting policies and controls in place to stop data loss are all essential components of an efficient DLP approach.

- **Data Identification and Classification:** To identify, manage, and safeguard sensitive data, including PII or intellectual property, DLP solutions depend on precise data classification.

- Establishing explicit DLP policies that specify authorized data usage and sharing criteria is the first step in creating and enforcing policies. Compliance is ensured by automated enforcement techniques including encryption or blockage of outgoing data.

- **Content Analysis and Filtering:** DLP systems examine data while it's in transit and at rest using content analysis to find keywords or patterns that point to the existence of sensitive data.

Avoiding Unauthorized Access and Insider Threats

Whether intentional or unintentional, insider threats pose a serious risk to data security. By monitoring and limiting data access and transmission, DLP systems assist in reducing these threats.

- **User activity Monitoring:** DLP systems monitor

and examine user activity, highlighting questionable actions including bulk file transfers, odd access patterns, or illegal data downloads.

- Role-based access control, or RBAC, restricts access to data according to job function, guaranteeing that workers only access information necessary for their positions.

- The danger of unintentional data loss due to carelessness or ignorance is decreased by educating staff members on security procedures and best practices for data protection.

Best Practices and DLP Tools

An organization's data protection capabilities are strengthened by putting DLP systems into place and following best practices, which also ensures regulatory compliance and guards against data breaches.

- **Endpoint DLP:** Prevents unwanted data exfiltration by monitoring and managing data transfer on endpoints, including email and USB drives.
- **Network DLP:** Examines network traffic and

quarantines or blocks sensitive information before it leaves the company's boundaries.

- By keeping an eye out for unwanted access or sharing of data on cloud storage, apps, and file-sharing platforms, Cloud DLP ensures data security in cloud environments.

- Frequent Compliance Checks and Audits: Regularly reviewing DLP policies and controls helps guarantee that data protection plans continue to be efficient and compliant with legal mandates like the CCPA, GDPR, and HIPAA.

A strong cybersecurity strategy is built on data security and encryption, which protect data against theft, alteration, and unwanted access. Organizations can preserve regulatory compliance and safeguard sensitive data by putting modern encryption techniques into practice, establishing effective DLP procedures, and adhering to data protection principles.

CHAPTER 7

Organizations are constantly at risk from cyber enemies in today's digital environment. Minimizing harm and guaranteeing a speedy recovery depend on efficient incident response (IR) and management. Planning, identifying, containing, and recovering from security incidents are the core goals of incident response in order to preserve business continuity. From planning and event detection to containment, recovery, and establishing a robust cybersecurity posture, this chapter covers all the important facets of incident response.

7.1 Planning for Incident Response

The first step in getting an organization ready for cybersecurity issues is incident response planning. Organizations can minimize possible damage and ensure coordinated actions across teams by acting quickly with a well-defined response strategy.

Establishing an Incident Response Strategy

The identification, management, and mitigation of cybersecurity incidents can be done in an orderly and controlled manner with the use of an incident response plan (IRP).

- The IRP's objective is to provide a complete guide for handling incidents in an efficient manner. It outlines specific procedures for detecting risks, containing incidents, and resuming activities.
- The response's scope, including systems, data, and locations, should be included in the plan. It should also include important goals like minimizing data loss, safeguarding customer information, and maintaining business continuity.
- **Procedures for Communication:** Clear channels of communication and protocols for alerting management, legal teams, and possibly impacted customers should be part of the IRP.

An incident response team's (IRT) function

Executing the incident response plan (IRP), organizing activities, and overseeing the issue's lifespan are the responsibilities of an incident response team (IRT).

- **The IRT's composition**: Executive decision-makers, PR and media personnel, legal counsel, and IT security experts are frequently included in the IRT. Every member has distinct duties and obligations.
- The IRT's responsibilities include: Throughout the situation, the team updates stakeholders, starts response procedures, and performs threat assessments. They are also in charge of recording the steps done to make post-event analysis easier.
- **Drills and Training:** Frequent simulation and training exercises assist guarantee that the IRT is ready for a variety of situations. Using realistic attack simulations to test the team's reactivity enhances their capacity to handle actual situations.

Important Elements of an Incident Response Plan

The foundation for handling security incidents is established by an incident response policy (IRP), which also formalizes the incident response procedure.

- The policy ought to specify precisely what qualifies as a security event and categorize them according to their level of severity. Data exfiltration, virus infection, and illegal access are a few examples.

- **Procedures for Escalation:** By establishing escalation pathways, major incidents are promptly reported to upper management, facilitating prompt resource mobilization and decision-making.

- **Requirements for Documentation:** Accurate documentation of incidents is necessary for learning from incidents, internal recordkeeping, and legal compliance. Every activity, conversation, and result ought to be documented.

7.2 Finding and Stopping Incidents

In incident response, early event detection and containment are essential measures. Early diagnosis and containment lessens the possible effects on finances, operations, and reputation.

A combination of threat intelligence and indicators of compromise (IoCs)

Forensic evidence of a possible breach or malicious activity is known as an Indicator of Compromise (IoC).

- Unusual login patterns, unexpected outgoing data transfers, modifications to system files, and new registry keys are examples of common IoCs. Early detection of possible threats is made possible by the recognition of IoCs.

- **Threat Intelligence's Function:** Threat intelligence gives organizations the most recent information on new risks, allowing them to identify and get ready for possible attacks. Governmental organizations, industry associations, and security companies can all provide intelligence.

- **Automated IoC Detection:** Endpoint Detection and

Response (EDR) tools and Security Information and Event Management (SIEM) systems can automatically identify IoCs and notify the IRT of any suspicious activity.

First Reaction: Recognition and Restrictions

As soon as an incident is discovered, it must be immediately contained in order to reduce damage and stop it from spreading.

- **Identification Steps:** By examining IoCs and performing preliminary evaluations, the IRT should confirm the incident. Comprehending the extent and characteristics of the threat aids in directing containment tactics.
- **Containment Strategies:** There are two types of containment: short-term (such separating compromised systems) and long-term (like redesigning systems to eliminate vulnerabilities). Examples include banning malicious IP addresses, disconnecting compromised computers, and disabling impacted accounts.

- **Interaction While Containing:** The IRT should maintain in touch with pertinent parties during the containment process to update them on developments and anticipated resolution dates.

Root Cause Analysis and Forensics

By determining the attack's source, methodology, and effects, forensics and root cause analysis offer vital information for averting such occurrences in the future.

- **Forensic Data Collection:** To examine the incident and comprehend the actions of the attacker, the IRT collects digital evidence such as logs, system snapshots, and memory dumps.
- Organizations can resolve the underlying problem by determining the root cause, which could be a phishing email, a misconfigured server, or an unpatched vulnerability.
- **Maintaining Documentation for Legal or Compliance Requirements:** Forensic data could occasionally be needed for legal or regulatory reasons. Evidence must be kept safe and undisturbed

for possible legal action or regulatory assessment.

7.3 Post-Incident Analysis and Recovery

The organization must concentrate on system restoration, incident review, and strengthening cybersecurity protections after the issue has been contained. In order to ensure long-term resilience and reduce future vulnerabilities, recovery and post-incident analysis are essential.

Procedures for System Restoration and Revalidation

The business must return the impacted systems to normal operations after the threat has been eliminated, making sure that all evidence of the occurrence has been eliminated.

- **System Restoration:** In order to remove all traces of the assault, it is frequently required to rebuild or restore systems from clean backups. Reinstalling operating systems, adjusting security settings, and installing patches could all be part of this procedure.
- **Clean Systems Validation:** Systems should undergo

thorough testing to make sure they are safe and malware-free before being reconnected to the network. Penetration testing and vulnerability scans are standard procedures to confirm system integrity.

- **Reconnecting to networks gradually:** IT staff can react swiftly if problems are found by reintroducing recovered systems to the network gradually while keeping an eye out for any lingering indications of compromise.

Takeaways and Enhancements to the Process

Organizations might find weaknesses in their response strategy and enhance future incident handling practices by analyzing the incident.

- **Meetings for Post-Incident Reviews:** To examine the incident, record findings, and pinpoint the response process's advantages and disadvantages, the IRT holds a review meeting.
- The IRP should be updated to reflect the lessons learned from the incident. This includes adding new IoCs, improving processes, and revising containment

and recovery plans as necessary.

- **Recommendations and Instruction:** Staff members' security awareness is raised and they are better equipped to identify and handle similar situations in the future when they are given access to incident insights.

Developing a Cybersecurity Posture That Is Resilient

Organizations can better resist and recover from such attacks when they have a robust cybersecurity posture. This calls for strong defenses, constant refinement, and a proactive response to new threats.

- The process of actively looking for threats that might evade conventional security measures is known as "proactive threat hunting." Organizations can identify dangers before they become more serious by routinely examining network traffic, logs, and other signs.

- **Putting Cybersecurity Best Practices into Practice:** Using best practices like network segmentation, frequent patching, and multi-factor authentication (MFA) lowers vulnerabilities and restricts the ability of attackers to take advantage of flaws.

- **Working with Industry Peers:** By taking part in information-sharing programs and working with industry peers, companies can get important insights on threat trends and successful defense tactics, which will help them become more resilient overall.

Organizations may effectively detect, contain, and recover from cybersecurity problems by implementing a systematic incident response and management approach. Through resilience-building and ongoing improvement, a well-prepared organization not only reduces possible harms but also strengthens its capacity to withstand future attacks. Advanced threat detection and response strategies that bolster an organization's defense capabilities will be examined in the upcoming chapter.

CHAPTER 8

LEGAL, ETHICAL, AND COMPLIANCE CONCERNS

The significance of following the law and moral principles to safeguard people and companies is increasing along with global worries about cybersecurity. Building a reliable and legally sound cybersecurity system requires adherence to legislation, knowledge of the legal environment, and respecting ethical obligations. This chapter explores the important facets of cybersecurity compliance, legal frameworks, and ethical considerations.

8.1 Being Aware of Cybersecurity Laws

Organizations must adhere to regulatory frameworks and regulations in order to safeguard sensitive information, secure their systems, and respect user privacy. Respecting these rules guarantees accountability and reduces risk.

GDPR, or the General Data Protection Regulation

A comprehensive data protection regulation known as the General Data Protection Regulation (GDPR) regulates how businesses in the European Union (EU) gather, handle, keep, and distribute personal data.

- **Scope and Applicability:** Regardless of the organization's location, GDPR is applicable to every entity that handles the personal data of EU citizens. Serious fines may result from noncompliance.

- **The fundamental tenets of GDPR are**: GDPR places a strong emphasis on confidentiality, integrity, accuracy, purpose limitation, and data minimization. In order to gather data, organizations must have express consent and be transparent about how they use that data.

- **The rights of data subjects:** Individuals have rights under the GDPR, such as the ability to view, amend, remove, and limit how their data is processed. Businesses must make sure they uphold these rights and make it easier for people to obtain their personal information when they ask for it.

- **Requirements for Notifying Data Breach:** GDPR

requires companies to notify the supervisory authority and impacted individuals within 72 hours of a data breach. This notice requirement promotes openness and prompt action.

HIPAA stands for Health Insurance Portability and Accountability Act.

HIPAA is a federal statute in the United States that aims to enhance healthcare data management and protect patient health information.

- **Protected Health Information (PHI):** HIPAA requires that PHI, such as insurance information, lab results, and medical histories, be protected. Strict privacy and security regulations must be followed by insurers, healthcare providers, and their business partners.
- **Privacy and Security Guidelines:** Standards for PHI protection, including technical, administrative, and physical measures, are established by the HIPAA Security Rule. Patients have control over their information thanks to the Privacy Rule, which

regulates how organizations may use and disclose PHI.

- The implementation of safe data storage, access controls, encryption, and employee training on managing sensitive information are all necessary for compliance. Fines, legal action, and harm to one's reputation may follow noncompliance.

- **Protocols for Data Breach:** According to HIPAA, covered organizations must notify the Department of Health and Human Services (HHS) and the impacted persons of any data breaches that impact more than 500 people.

PCI DSS, or Payment Card Industry Data Security Standard

A global standard called PCI DSS was developed to guarantee that credit card data is processed, stored, and sent securely.

- **Applicability and Requirements:** Businesses, financial institutions, and payment processors that accept credit card payments are all subject to PCI

DSS. Access control, vulnerability management, and a secure network design are all mandated by the standard.

- **PCI DSS Key Controls**: Encrypting cardholder data, limiting access to cardholder data, keeping an eye on network traffic, and maintaining secure systems and applications are essential criteria. Cardholders are shielded against fraud and identity theft by these precautions.

- **Annual Assessment of Compliance:** To confirm PCI DSS compliance, organizations must go through assessments on a regular basis. Employee training, vulnerability scans, and on-site assessments are a few examples of assessments.

- **Consequences of Non-Compliance:** Businesses that disregard PCI DSS risk fines from credit card networks and heightened regulatory attention, among other consequences.

8.2 Cybersecurity Laws and the Legal Framework

Organizations can avoid legal ramifications and strengthen their commitment to user data protection by being aware of cybersecurity rules and regulations.

Laws and Enforcement Regarding Cybercrime

Unauthorized access, data theft, malware dissemination, and other cyber offenses that endanger people and organizations are covered by cybercrime legislation.

- The CFAA (Computer Fraud and Abuse Act): Unauthorized access to computer systems is prohibited in the US by the CFAA, which makes it unlawful to take data or harm systems without authorization.
- The Convention on Cybercrime in Europe: A foundation for combating cybercrime worldwide is provided by the Convention on Cybercrime, also referred to as the Budapest Convention. It encourages international collaboration on investigations and enforcement.
- **Difficulties in Law Enforcement:** Because hackers sometimes act internationally, prosecuting cyber crimes can be difficult because of jurisdictional concerns. To effectively address cyber threats, law

enforcement agencies work together on a global scale.

- **New and Developing Cyberthreats:** In order to handle emerging dangers like ransomware and crimes involving cryptocurrencies, cybercrime laws are always changing. Together, lawmakers and cybersecurity specialists modify legislative frameworks to address new threats.

Data Protection Rights and Privacy Laws

Privacy laws, which emphasize the need to strike a balance between data use and user rights, regulate how businesses gather, utilize, and share people's personal information.

- The California Consumer Privacy Act, or CCPA, grants Californians the right to know what personal information is gathered, the power to request that data be deleted, and the choice to refuse data sales. It places a strong emphasis on data control and transparency.
- **Data Protection Rights Worldwide:** Nations that have enacted data protection laws that adhere to

GDPR principles, stressing the right to data privacy and requiring express user consent, include Brazil (LGPD), Australia (Privacy Act), and Japan (APPI).

- **Right to be Forgotten:** The "right to be forgotten," which is frequently included in privacy regulations, enables people to ask for their personal information to be deleted when it is no longer required. This privilege helps reduce the hazards associated with data retention while safeguarding people's privacy.

Global Cyber Law Compliance Challenges

As businesses grow internationally and are required to abide by a variety of regional legislation, compliance with cyber laws becomes increasingly complicated.

- **Data Transfers Across Borders:** The transmission of data outside of their jurisdiction without sufficient safeguards is restricted by regulations such as GDPR. Data transfers must adhere to international norms, which organizations must make sure of.
- **Differing Standards for Privacy:** While some areas place a higher priority on privacy, others place more

emphasis on intelligence collecting and data sharing. Multinational corporations must comprehend and adjust to different legal standards because this leads to legal issues.

- **Conflicts and Regulatory Overlap**: Numerous firms must balance compliance requirements and guarantee uniform security measures across all jurisdictions due to overlapping or conflicting rules.

8.3 Professional Responsibility and Ethics

Ethics are fundamental to cybersecurity because they help professionals make moral choices that safeguard people, businesses, and society as a whole.

Ethics's Function in Cybersecurity

The need to preserve trust, guarantee data confidentiality, and defend individual rights are all included in cybersecurity ethics.

- **Respecting User Privacy:** Because cybersecurity experts deal with sensitive data, they must protect user privacy and stop illegal data disclosure. Ethical behavior discourages data collection and surveillance that goes beyond what is required by law.

- **Accountability and Transparency:** Transparent communication with stakeholders about security threats, events, and policy changes is a key component of ethical cybersecurity practices, which also promote an accountable culture.

- The design of cybersecurity solutions should aim to prevent overreach, minimize harm to users, and steer clear of intrusive activities that violate people's rights.

Keeping Security and Privacy in Check

Since improved security may necessitate gathering and evaluating personal data, security and privacy are frequently at odds. Professionals in cybersecurity need to find a balance between protecting against attacks and maintaining privacy.

- **Reducing the amount of data collected:** By simply

gathering the information that is required, privacy risks and misuse potential are decreased. To preserve user privacy, cybersecurity teams should promote data minimization techniques.

- **Maintaining Data Integrity:** The accuracy and integrity of data must be preserved by cybersecurity initiatives, preventing data manipulation or needless disclosure of personal information.

- **Ethical Conundrums:** When security requirements and user privacy clash, professionals may encounter moral conundrums. Codes of conduct and ethical frameworks offer direction on how to act appropriately in such circumstances.

Professional Standards and Conduct Codes

Professional codes of conduct set expectations for cybersecurity practitioners' moral conduct, honesty, and accountability.

- **International Codes of Conduct:** Codes of ethics that outline the values of honesty, equity, and privacy protection are provided by organizations like

ISACA, SANS, and ISC².

- **Employer Expectations and Policies:** Numerous companies have internal codes of conduct that require staff members to perform their jobs in an ethical and responsible manner. A culture of security and trust is fostered by these regulations.

- **Ongoing Awareness and Education:** Professionals in cybersecurity should remain up to date on the latest ethical dilemmas and difficulties in the industry. Professionals' capacity to make moral decisions is enhanced by regular training and involvement in ethical debates.

Firms that want to safeguard data, preserve privacy, and promote public trust must conform to cybersecurity legislation, legal frameworks, and ethical standards. In order to safely safeguard systems while upholding user rights and legal requirements, cybersecurity specialists are essential in traversing these intricate domains. We will examine cutting-edge security procedures that improve the organization's cybersecurity posture and resilience in the upcoming chapter.

CHAPTER 9

CYBERSECURITY'S EMERGING TECHNOLOGIES

The technology used to combat cyberthreats is always changing along with them. By strengthening threat detection, enhancing data integrity, and changing encryption techniques, emerging technologies like artificial intelligence, blockchain, and quantum computing are revolutionizing cybersecurity. This chapter examines these state-of-the-art developments and their possible effects, difficulties, and uses in cybersecurity.

9.1 Machine learning and artificial intelligence

By improving an organization's capacity to identify, stop, and react to cyberthreats, artificial intelligence (AI) and machine learning (ML) are revolutionizing cybersecurity. These technologies provide previously unheard-of assistance in detecting vulnerabilities and anticipating assaults due to their capacity to process enormous volumes of data quickly.

AI-Powered Threat Identification and Reaction

AI is being utilized more and more to detect cyberthreats by using complex algorithms that can spot trends that point to illicit activities.

- **Automated Threat Analysis:** To identify irregularities and possible dangers, AI systems can examine system logs, user activity, and network traffic. AI can collect and analyze data in real time, providing quicker and more precise insights than traditional detection methods.

- **Predictive Capabilities:** AI can anticipate possible security events by using past data, offering proactive protections against both known and unknown threats. This prediction skill is particularly useful for spotting evolving advanced persistent threats (APTs).

- **Automated Incident Response:** AI-powered solutions are able to operate on their own in response to threats by identifying and removing impacted systems, notifying response teams, and even installing updates. Response times are sped up and less manual involvement is required thanks to this automation.

Anomaly Detection with Machine Learning

A kind of artificial intelligence called machine learning is very useful for spotting odd activity in networks and systems since it focuses on finding aberrant patterns by learning from data.

- **Behavioral Analysis:** ML algorithms are used to examine the behavior of entities and users, identifying deviations and learning what is deemed "normal." This is helpful in identifying unwanted access and insider threats.

- **The adaptive detection method:** Organizations can identify new attack vectors thanks to machine learning models, which, in contrast to static rule-based systems, adapt to new threat patterns. For instance, using metadata and minor language clues, machine learning can detect phishing emails.

- **False Positives Have Dropped:** In cybersecurity, handling false positives when harmless behavior is mistakenly reported as malicious is one of the biggest problems. Over time, machine learning (ML) improves detection models, producing more accurate findings and lowering the noise that security professionals must deal with.

AI's Risks and Difficulties in Cybersecurity

Although AI significantly improves cybersecurity, it also poses new dangers and concerns.

- **AI Prejudice and Data Accuracy**: The caliber and variety of training data have a significant impact on AI efficacy. AI models may overlook some risks or mistakenly perceive harmless behaviors as malevolent if biased or insufficient data is employed.
- **Adversarial Assault:** Cybercriminals are creating methods to use adversarial assaults to take advantage of weaknesses in AI models. For example, attackers can circumvent threat detection systems by subtly altering input data to trick an AI model.

- **Ethical and Privacy Issues:** Large datasets that may contain sensitive user information are frequently needed by AI-based systems, which raises questions around data privacy and regulatory compliance. Businesses need to make sure that the use of AI complies with privacy regulations and ethical norms.

9.2 Security using Blockchain

Data integrity, secure authentication, and Internet of Things (IoT) security can all be improved using blockchain, a decentralized and impenetrable ledger platform. Blockchain has a lot of potential for cybersecurity since it can offer transparent and safe record-keeping.

Data Integrity with Blockchain

Blockchain is a great tool for guaranteeing the validity and integrity of data because of its immutability.

- **Records that are resistant to tampering:** Data cannot be changed once it has been added to a blockchain without the network's members' consent.

Blockchain is therefore perfect for preserving the accuracy of important documents, such supply chain logs or financial transactions.

- There are auditable trails: Blockchain enables businesses to track any changes back to their original source by producing an auditable and transparent record of data revisions. In sectors like finance and healthcare, where data authenticity and accuracy are critical, this skill is vital.

- **Provenance and Verification of Data:** Blockchain technology can be used to confirm the legitimacy of data by confirming its source. This is especially important for protecting intellectual property and confirming digital identities.

Decentralized Access Control and Authentication

Blockchain reduces dependency on conventional central authentication systems that are susceptible to breaches by providing new techniques for secure and decentralized authentication.

- **Self-Sovereign identification:** By removing the

need for central databases that hackers find appealing, blockchain technology allows people to manage their own digital identities through self-sovereign identification (SSI) systems.

- **Multi-Factor Authentication (MFA) with Blockchain**: Decentralized multi-factor authentication can be supported by blockchain-based authentication solutions, improving security without the need for centralized administration. This strategy reduces the risks brought on by single points of failure.

- Role-based access control, or RBAC, is a way for blockchain technology to manage permissions. It creates an immutable record of access privileges, which increases accountability and decreases unlawful access.

The Function of Blockchain in IoT Security

IoT devices, which are frequently subject to assaults because of their low processing power and lack of standardized security measures, can be secured thanks to blockchain's decentralized architecture.

- Decentralized IoT networks can be supported by blockchain technology, which lowers reliance on central servers and lowers the possibility of a single point of failure.

- **Secure Device-to-Device Communication:** By logging each device's distinct identification on the blockchain, verifying interactions, and blocking unwanted access, blockchain technology guarantees secure communication between Internet of Things devices.

- **Firmware and Update Verification:** Blockchain can be used to validate firmware updates, protecting IoT devices from malware injection attacks by guaranteeing that only genuine software is installed.

9.3 Cybersecurity and Quantum Computing

Although it is still in its infancy, quantum computing offers cybersecurity both enormous prospects and difficulties. The development of new quantum-safe algorithms is necessary because quantum computing has the potential to crack popular encryption techniques due to its exponentially faster ability to solve complicated mathematical problems than conventional computers.

Quantum Computing's Effect on Encryption

The enormous processing power of quantum computing may make conventional encryption techniques outdated, which would be extremely dangerous for data security.

- **Public-Key Cryptography Threat:** The mathematical issues that underlie public-key cryptography, such RSA and ECC, can be resolved by quantum computers at a rate never before possible. This could make protected communications susceptible by allowing attackers to crack encryption keys.
- **The effect on secure communications is as follows:** There would be a risk to sensitive information that is currently shielded by conventional encryption techniques, such as government communications and financial transactions. To protect data in the future, organizations need to start getting ready for a

post-quantum cryptography environment.

- **Prolonged Data Security**: Once quantum computers achieve a certain level of capacity, data that has been encrypted today may become exposed because quantum computing may retroactively defeat encryption. To stop future data breaches, organizations need to think about long-term data protection measures.

Quantum-Safe Standards and Algorithms

Researchers are creating quantum-safe algorithms to fend against quantum computer attacks in response to the possible threat posed by quantum computing.

- **PQC, or post-quantum cryptography:** The purpose of PQC algorithms is to protect against quantum attacks. To assist businesses in making the switch to quantum-resistant encryption, groups like the National Institute of Standards and Technology (NIST) are standardizing these algorithms.
- **The Cryptography Based on Lattice Framework:** Lattice-based cryptography, one of the most popular

methods for quantum-safe encryption, is based on intricate mathematical structures that are difficult for quantum computers to understand.

- **Models of Hybrid Encryption:** Organizations may use hybrid models that mix conventional and quantum-safe encryption to add an extra degree of protection until quantum-safe standards are completely developed.

Getting Ready for the Quantum Era

Establishing resilience against quantum-enabled risks and implementing quantum-resistant activities are essential steps in preparing organizations for the upcoming change.

- **Quantum Readiness Assessments:** To determine which assets need quantum-safe encryption and to comprehend their vulnerability to quantum threats, organizations can conduct quantum readiness assessments.
- **Research and development investments:** It's critical to keep up with developments in post-quantum cryptography and quantum computing.

To stay on the cutting edge of quantum-safe technologies, organizations should think about funding research and development.

- **Working together with governments and industry:** Establishing and implementing quantum-safe encryption standards will require cooperation between governments, industry, and standard-setting organizations as quantum computer capabilities develop.

New technologies like blockchain, quantum computing, and artificial intelligence are changing the cybersecurity scene by posing both new difficulties and improved possibilities. Organizations hoping to maintain strong cybersecurity in a quickly changing digital world will need to stay ahead of these developments and comprehend their possible effects. Best practices for incorporating these technologies into an all-encompassing cybersecurity plan will be covered in the upcoming chapter.

CHAPTER 10

CYBERSECURITY'S FUTURE

The future of cybersecurity seems to be both difficult and revolutionary as digital environments change and cyberthreats get more complex. To be resilient against new threats, organizations will need to invest in skills, maintain agility, and foster a security-focused culture. The development of critical skills, the significance of cultivating a cybersecurity culture at all organizational levels, and major trends in cybersecurity are all covered in this chapter.

10.1 Cybersecurity Trends

Organizations must take a proactive approach to cybersecurity if they want to stay ahead in a world that is becoming more interconnected. The main trends influencing the sector are proactive tactics, executive-level cybersecurity priorities, and resilience development.

The Transition to Predictive and Proactive Security

In the past, cybersecurity was mostly concerned with responding to security breaches after they happened. The focus of cybersecurity in the future, however, will be on proactive and predictive strategies that use cutting-edge technologies to foresee and eliminate dangers before they materialize.

- **Threat Intelligence and Analytics:** Organizations can take preventative measures by using threat intelligence data and analytics to learn about potential vulnerabilities and threat patterns.

- **The use of predictive technologies:** To anticipate and thwart threats, cybersecurity technologies are incorporating machine learning and artificial intelligence. Algorithms for anomaly detection, for example, spot strange trends in network traffic and notify security teams of possible breaches before harm is done.

- **Automation and Orchestration of Response:** Automated incident response systems minimize possible harm by cutting down on the amount of time required to contain threats. These tools increase the productivity of security teams and optimize workflows; they are frequently included in security orchestration, automation, and response (SOAR) platforms.

Making cybersecurity a top priority in the boardroom

Cybersecurity is no longer only an IT problem; board members and senior leadership now view it as a strategic concern. Executive executives must support cybersecurity measures since a single breach can have serious operational, financial, and reputational repercussions.

- **Management of Risk at the Executive Level:** Senior executives and board members are now actively involved in evaluating and controlling cyber risks. This change highlights how crucial cybersecurity is to corporate governance and overall risk management.
- **Investments and Budgets for Cybersecurity:** Organizations are investing more in cybersecurity as

cyber dangers increase. It is now considered necessary rather than optional to invest in cybersecurity personnel, equipment, and training.

- **Pressures from Regulation and Compliance:** Organizations must guarantee adherence to cybersecurity standards in the face of more stringent rules and greater responsibility, which calls for board-level involvement. Additionally, this approach builds trust with partners and customers and enhances an organization's reputation.

A Greater Emphasis on Cyber Resilience

The capacity to endure and swiftly bounce back from cyberattacks while reducing operational disruption is resilience. Strategies for cyber resilience have an emphasis on continuity and quick recovery in addition to defense.

- **Plans for Incident Response and Recovery:** It is essential to have a strong incident response plan. Organizations can better prepare for real-world catastrophes by routinely testing these plans through tabletop exercises and simulations.

- **Constructing Redundancy:** Organizations can continue to function even in the case of an attack by implementing redundancies and backups in vital systems. Cloud-based backups and geographically dispersed data centers are examples of this.

- **Integration of Business Continuity:** Beyond technology, cyber resilience necessitates an integrated strategy that complements business continuity strategies. Organizations may safeguard their most important operations and services both during and after an incident by making sure that their cybersecurity and continuity plans are in sync.

10.2 Development of Cybersecurity Skills

There is a pressing need for a trained workforce that can handle these issues as cyber threats become more complicated. The sector must prioritize skill development since the need for cybersecurity specialists is still greater than the supply.

Essential Competencies for Cybersecurity Experts

Professionals in cybersecurity require a combination of technical know-how and soft skills to thrive as the field becomes more complex. Navigating the complex nature of cyber threats requires an understanding of the numerous cybersecurity disciplines.

- **Proficiency in technical aspects:** Fundamental knowledge of network security, encryption, and threat analysis is required of cybersecurity experts. It is crucial to have knowledge of operating systems, particularly Linux, network protocols, and programming languages like Python.

- **The ability to think critically and solve problems:** Finding patterns in big datasets and resolving complicated issues are frequent tasks in cybersecurity. Professionals with analytical abilities are better able to evaluate circumstances fast and reach well-informed conclusions.

- **Communication Proficiency:** It's a useful ability to explain technical ideas to stakeholders who aren't technical. Effective communication guarantees that CEOs are aware of security threats, allowing for well-informed leadership decision-making.

Programs for Certification and Training

Continuing education courses and certifications are essential for preserving cybersecurity proficiency. Staying current with the newest technologies and strategies requires ongoing study as new threats appear.

Professionals can confirm their expertise with the help of popular cybersecurity certifications such as CompTIA Security+, Certified Ethical Hacker (CEH), and Certified Information Systems Security Professional (CISSP). Additionally beneficial qualifications include specialized certificates in cloud security (CCSP), governance (CISM), and auditing (CISA).

- **Practical Instruction and Labs:** In cybersecurity, real-world experience is crucial. Hack The Box and TryHackMe are two platforms that provide simulated attack environments so that experts can practice and test their skills in real-world situations.
- **Employer-Sponsored Training:** Because they understand how important skilled employees are to preserving a safe workplace, many companies fund

cybersecurity training and certification initiatives.

Education and Awareness on Cybersecurity

In addition to technical proficiency, cybersecurity awareness needs to be ingrained in every position in a company. One of the main reasons for breaches is human error, which may be avoided by teaching staff members about security best practices.

- **End-User Training Programs:** It is crucial to provide regular training on social engineering, phishing, and safe online conduct. These initiatives can assist staff members in identifying typical dangers and steering clear of dangerous conduct.
- **Campaigns to Raise Awareness of Security:** Organizations can reinforce recommended practices and remind employees of cybersecurity regulations through interactive training, posters, and email notifications.
- **Key Role Specific Training:** Because they deal with sensitive data, employees in the legal, HR, and finance departments could need extra training.

Role-specific hazards are addressed by customized programs, which also improve company security as a whole.

10.3 Establishing a Culture of Cybersecurity

Establishing a cybersecurity culture within a company guarantees that security is given top priority at all levels. Long-term success depends on having a strong cybersecurity culture that encourages alertness, accountability, and group responsibility.

Raising Awareness on All Fronts

Raising awareness throughout the company makes sure that everyone, from CEOs to entry-level workers, is aware of their cybersecurity responsibilities. The organization's general philosophy should incorporate security, not just the IT department.

- **Training for the entire organization:** Training programs that are thorough and consistent aid in establishing cybersecurity as a shared responsibility.

Employee vigilance is maintained by regular information on changing dangers.

- **Engagement Activities:** Employees can learn about security in a more memorable and interesting way by participating in gamified training sessions, cybersecurity quizzes, and phishing simulations.

- **Leadership's Function in Raising Awareness:** A culture of accountability is strengthened and employees are encouraged to take security seriously when managers and leaders stress the significance of cybersecurity.

Business Process Integration with Security

Security ought to be a key consideration in corporate choices and procedures rather than an afterthought. Organizations can reduce risks and make sure that security measures complement business goals by integrating security into workflows.

- It is imperative for software development organizations to integrate security into the software development lifecycle (SDLC) through the use of secure development practices. Techniques like penetration testing, vulnerability assessments, and code reviews enhance an application's security from the ground up.

- **Management of Vendors and Third Parties**: Since vendors frequently have access to private information and systems, it is essential to evaluate their cybersecurity policies. Third-party risks are reduced when security factors are incorporated into vendor evaluation procedures.

- **Frequent Risk Evaluations:** Regular risk assessments ensure that security is maintained as company operations change by assisting businesses in identifying and addressing possible weaknesses in business processes.

Methods for Successful Long-Term Cybersecurity

It takes dedication, strategic planning, and ongoing development to maintain a cybersecurity culture. To remain resilient in the face of a shifting threat landscape, organizations need to make continuous investments in initiatives.

- **Ongoing Education and Development:** The field of cybersecurity is dynamic, and maintaining security necessitates ongoing change. Professionals should be open to new methods and encouraged to pursue continuing education by their organizations.

- **Mechanisms for Employee Feedback:** Giving staff members a forum to voice their opinions about security procedures can result in insightful discoveries and advancements. This strategy also encourages participation and a sense of responsibility in cybersecurity maintenance.

- **Assessing and Incentives for Security Efforts**: A cybersecurity culture can be strengthened by praising and recognizing staff members who exhibit excellent security procedures. Recognizing staff members who disclose phishing attempts or other possible security risks may fall under this category.

In summary, firms must invest in talent development, embrace proactive security measures, and cultivate a culture that places a high priority on security at all levels if they hope to succeed in the future of cybersecurity. These procedures will be the cornerstone of a robust, safe, and flexible cybersecurity posture as the digital environment develops further. In order to assist firms plan and implement strong defenses in a constantly changing threat environment, the following chapter will concentrate on creating an integrated cybersecurity strategy.

ABOUT THE AUTHOR

 Author and thought leader in the IT field Taylor Royce is well known. He has a two-decade career and is an expert at tech trend analysis and forecasting, which enables a wide audience to understand complicated concepts.

Royce's considerable involvement in the IT industry stemmed from his passion with technology, which he developed during his computer science studies. He has extensive knowledge of the industry because of his experience in both software development and strategic consulting.

Known for his research and lucidity, he has written multiple best-selling books and contributed to esteemed tech periodicals. Translations of Royce's books throughout the world demonstrate his impact.

Royce is a well-known authority on emerging technologies

and their effects on society, frequently requested as a speaker at international conferences and as a guest on tech podcasts. He promotes the development of ethical technology, emphasizing problems like data privacy and the digital divide.

In addition, with a focus on sustainable industry growth, Royce mentors upcoming tech experts and supports IT education projects. Taylor Royce is well known for his ability to combine analytical thinking with technical know-how. He sees a time when technology will ethically benefit humanity.

www.ingramcontent.com/pod-product-compliance
Lightning Source LLC
La Vergne TN
LVHW051657050326
832903LV00032B/3860